**Sports Illustrated KIDS**

# FOOTBALL PARTY RECIPES

## DELICIOUS IDEAS FOR THE BIG EVENT

by Katrina Jorgensen

CAPSTONE PRESS
a capstone imprint

Sports Illustrated Kids Football Cookbooks are published by Capstone Press,
1710 Roe Crest Drive, North Mankato, Minnesota 56003.
www.capstonepub.com

Sports Illustrated Kids is a trademark of Time Inc. Used with permission.

**Library of Congress Cataloging-in-Publication Data**
Jorgensen, Katrina, author.
  Football party recipes : delicious ideas for the big event / by Katrina Jorgensen.
     pages cm.—(Sports illustrated kids. Football cookbooks.)
  Summary: "A fun cookbook with recipes for a football party"—Provided
by publisher.
  Includes bibliographical references.
  ISBN 978-1-4914-2136-9 (library binding)
1.  Snack foods—Juvenile literature. 2.  Children's parties—Juvenile literature.  I. Title
  TX740.J67 2015
  641.5'68—dc23                                   2014034067

**Editorial Credits**
Anthony Wacholtz, editor; Kyle Grenz, designer; Eric Gohl, media researcher;
Laura Manthe, production specialist; Marcy Morin, scheduler;
Sarah Schuette, photo stylist

**Photo Credits**
All images by Capstone Studio: Karon Dubke. Author photo by
STILLCODA Photography.

The author dedicates this book to her great-grandmother Dorothy, who inspired her
to explore the culinary world.

Printed in Canada.
092014      008478FRS15

# TABLE OF CONTENTS

# Score With Your Football Party!

Ready to make the big play? Get your football party hopping with a selection of eats and treats. Team up any of the appetizers, main courses, desserts, and drinks to make the perfect formation. You'll be sure to kick off your party with tantalizing tastes! Get started by gathering the supplies and ingredients. See each recipe for the full list of what you'll need to start cooking.

| PREP TIME | the amount of time it takes to prepare ingredients before cooking |
| --- | --- |
| INACTIVE PREP TIME | the amount of time it takes to indirectly prepare ingredients before cooking, such as allowing dough to rise |
| COOK TIME | the amount of time it takes to cook a recipe after preparing the ingredients |

## Conversions

Using metric tools? No problem! These metric conversions will make your recipe measure up.

## Temperature

| Fahrenheit | Celsius |
| --- | --- |
| 325° | 160° |
| 350° | 180° |
| 375° | 190° |
| 400° | 200° |
| 425° | 220° |
| 450° | 230° |

## Measurements

| 1/4 teaspoon | 1.25 grams or milliliters |
| --- | --- |
| 1/2 teaspoon | 2.5 g or mL |
| 1 teaspoon | 5 g or mL |
| 1 tablespoon | 15 g or mL |
| 1/4 cup | 57 g (dry) or 60 mL (liquid) |
| 1/3 cup | 75 g (dry) or 80 mL (liquid) |
| 1/2 cup | 114 g (dry) or 125 mL (liquid) |
| 2/3 cup | 150 g (dry) or 160 mL (liquid) |
| 3/4 cup | 170 g (dry) or 175 mL (liquid) |
| 1 cup | 227 g (dry) or 240 mL (liquid) |
| 1 quart | 950 mL |

blend—to mix together, sometimes using a blender

boil—to heat until large bubbles form on top of a liquid; the boiling point for water is 212°F (100°C)

chop—to cut into small pieces with a knife

dissolve—to incorporate a solid food into a liquid by melting or stirring

grate—to cut into small strips using a grater

knead—to mix dough by flattening it with the heel of your hand, folding it in half, pressing down again, and repeating several times; use flour on your work surface to prevent the dough from sticking

mash—to smash a soft food into a lumpy mixture

preheat—to turn the oven on ahead of time so it reaches the correct temperature before you are ready to bake

simmer—to cook foods in hot liquids kept just below the boiling point of water

slice—to cut into thin pieces with a knife

spread—to put a thin layer of a soft food onto another food

thaw—to bring frozen food to room temperature

**CALL AN AUDIBLE**

Not liking what you see at the start of the play? Make some changes in the recipe to have success against even the toughest defenses.

**Keep your eyes open for helpful and creative sidebars throughout the book. Switch up your recipes with Call an Audible ideas, and get insight from the expert with Coach's Tips!**

**COACH'S TIP**

Gain the edge in the kitchen with these cool tips, tricks, and techniques.

# Safety in the Kitchen

You can have fun in the kitchen and be safe too. Always start your recipes with clean hands, tools, and surfaces. Make sure you wash your hands and keep your tools and surfaces clean after handling raw meat. Use your knife carefully. Ask an adult for help when cutting food or handling hot dishes.

Just as football players need the right equipment to play their best, you'll need a variety of tools to tackle these recipes.

1. baking sheets
2. can opener
3. chef's knife
4. colander
5. cutting board
6. grater
7. 2-inch ice cream scoop
8. kitchen shears
9. large skillet
10. measuring cups
11. measuring spoons
12. mixing bowls
13. mixing spoon
14. pastry brush
15. rolling pin
16. slotted spoon
17. spatula
18. tongs
19. whisk

# SOFT PRETZEL BITES AND HONEY-MUSTARD DIPPING SAUCE

Delicious bite-sized pretzels are sure to score a touchdown with your crowd.

| | |
|---|---|
| **PREP TIME** | **1 HOUR** (½ HOUR INACTIVE) |
| **COOK TIME** | **30 MINUTES** (INACTIVE) |
| **MAKES** | **ABOUT 32 PRETZEL BITES** |

## Tools

- 3 saucepans
- 3 mixing bowls
- measuring spoons
- measuring cups
- damp kitchen towel
- chef's knife
- kitchen shears
- baking sheet
- parchment paper
- slotted spoon
- pastry brush

## Ingredients

**For the dough:**
- 2 tablespoons butter
- 1 packet instant yeast
- 1 pinch of salt
- 1 teaspoon honey
- 1 cup warm water
- 2½ cups flour, plus more for kneading
- vegetable oil spray

**For cooking:**
- 3 cups water
- ½ cup baking soda
- vegetable oil spray
- 6 tablespoons butter
- kosher salt, for sprinkling
- poppy seeds, for sprinkling
- sesame seeds, for sprinkling

**For the Honey Mustard Dip:**
- 1 cup coarse ground mustard
- ½ cup honey
- 1 teaspoon salt

1 Place 2 tablespoons butter in a saucepan and melt over low heat.

2 In a large mixing bowl, combine the butter, yeast, salt, honey, and warm water. Allow to sit for about 2 minutes.

3 Add the flour. Mix it well and turn the bowl upside down onto a floured surface. Knead the dough well with your hands for about 5 minutes, or until it is soft and smooth.

4 Spray the inside of a clean mixing bowl with vegetable oil spray and place the dough in the bowl. Cover with a clean damp cloth and allow to sit for 30 minutes to rise.

## COACH'S TIP

What's in a "pinch?" There is no spoon to measure this tiny amount. Whatever you can grab between your thumb and forefinger is the perfect measurement.

**5** Flour your surface again and place the dough ball on it. Knead for one minute and then cut the dough into six equal pieces.

**6** Roll the dough between your hands and the counter to make ropes about 12 inches long.

**7** Using kitchen shears, snip each rope into 12 equal pieces.

**8** Preheat oven to 400°F. Line baking sheet with parchment paper and set aside.

**9** Boil the water in a saucepan. Add baking soda and stir until it dissolves. Reduce the heat so it slowly simmers.

**10** Drop the dough bites in the saucepan six at a time. Let them cook for about 30 seconds.

**11** Remove the dough bites from the pan with a slotted spoon. Place the bites about ¼-inch apart on the baking sheet. Sprinkle with salt. Add seeds for extra flavor if desired.

**12** Bake for about 15 minutes or until they are golden brown.

**13** Meanwhile, melt 6 tablespoons butter in a saucepan over low heat.

**14** Remove from oven and brush with melted butter using the pastry brush. Allow to cool for about 10 minutes before serving.

## CALL AN AUDIBLE

For a little extra flavor in your pasta, add sliced summer squash in step 3 and sliced cherry tomatoes in step 5.

**For the dipping sauce:**

**1** Combine all of the ingredients in the mixing bowl.

**2** Taste the mixture and add more honey or mustard if needed. Serve alongside your pretzel bites.

# SWEET & SALTY SNACK MIX

Nuts and pretzels come together with sweet and salty flavors for a pregame snack.

| PREP TIME | 10 MINUTES |
| --- | --- |
| COOK TIME | 15 MINUTES |
| MAKES | ABOUT 4 CUPS |

## Tools

- large baking sheet
- parchment paper
- measuring cups
- measuring spoons
- small saucepan
- large mixing bowl
- bowl scraper

## Ingredients

- 1 tablespoon butter
- ¼ cup water
- ½ cup sugar
- ¾ teaspoon salt
- ½ teaspoon pepper
- 2 cups mixed nuts, unsalted
- 2 cups pretzels

1. Preheat oven to 350°F. Line a baking sheet with parchment paper and set aside.

2. In the saucepan, combine the butter, water, and sugar. Place over medium heat. Stir to dissolve the sugar and simmer for 1 minute. Set aside.

3. Combine the remaining ingredients in the mixing bowl.

4. Slowly pour the butter, water, and sugar over the nut mixture and stir gently with your bowl scraper. Be careful not to break the pretzels.

5. Pour the nut mixture onto the baking sheet. Carefully spread the mixture out into a single layer.

6. Bake for 10 minutes. Then remove from the oven and stir the nut mixture, keeping it in a single layer.

7. Bake an additional 5 minutes. Allow to cool for 15 minutes before serving.

## CALL AN AUDIBLE

Want to spice up the recipe? Add ½ teaspoon cayenne pepper and 1 teaspoon cumin in step 2.

# FOOTBALL BACON CHEESEBALL

Before the game's opening kickoff, you can kick off your party with a cheesy appetizer.

**PREP TIME** | **25 MINUTES**

**COOK TIME** | **2 HOURS (INACTIVE)**

**SERVES** | **6 TO 8 PEOPLE**

## Tools

- large skillet
- tongs
- paper towels
- chef's knife
- cutting board
- large mixing bowl
- measuring cups
- grater
- bowl scraper
- plastic wrap
- serving plate

## Ingredients

- 8 ounces bacon
- 4 ounces white cheddar cheese
- 3 green onions
- 8 ounces cream cheese, at room temperature
- 1 teaspoon pepper
- crackers, chips, and veggies for serving

1 Place bacon in skillet over medium heat and cook until crispy on both sides, using tongs to flip. Be careful of spatters!

2 Set the cooked bacon on a small stack of paper towels to drain extra fat. Allow to cool for 10 minutes.

3 Coarsely chop bacon into bite-sized pieces and place half in the mixing bowl. Set the rest aside.

## CALL AN AUDIBLE

Not a fan of bacon? Sub in 2 cups of chopped pecans instead. Skip steps 1 and 2, and mix in half the pecans in step 3. Use the remaining half to cover the cheeseball in step 8.

**4** Cut one slice of the white cheddar cheese and set aside. Grate the rest and place in the mixing bowl.

**5** Chop the green onions finely and add to mixing bowl.

**6** In the mixing bowl, add cream cheese and pepper. Mix well with bowl scraper.

**7** Scrape the cheese mixture onto a large sheet of plastic wrap. Using the plastic to avoid getting your hands cheesy, shape the mixture into a round ball.

**8** Refrigerate the plastic-wrapped ball for 2 hours.

**9** While the ball is still in the plastic, form into a football shape the best you can. Remove the plastic and place on a serving plate.

**10** Cover the cheeseball with the remaining bacon.

**11** Remember the slice of white cheddar cheese you set aside in step 4? Cut that piece into small slices for the laces. Place on the cheeseball.

**12** Serve with a variety of crackers, vegetables, and chips.

# PEACH BBQ MEATBALLS

Deliciously sweet and tangy, these meatballs are a snap to make and sure to be a party pleaser!

**PREP TIME** 45 MINUTES

**COOK TIME** 4 HOURS (INACTIVE)

**MAKES** ABOUT 25 2-INCH MEATBALLS

## Tools

- 1-quart saucepan
- measuring cups
- mixing spoon
- large mixing bowl
- measuring spoons
- fork
- 2-inch scoop
- 2 baking sheets
- 10-inch skillet
- tongs
- 3-quart slow cooker

## Ingredients

- 1 pound lean ground beef
- 1 pound ground pork
- 2 eggs
- 1 cup bread crumbs
- ½ cup milk
- 1 teaspoon garlic powder
- 1 teaspoon onion powder
- 1½ teaspoons salt
- 1 teaspoon pepper
- pinch red pepper flakes
- 2 tablespoons oil

**For the sauce:**
- 24-ounce bottle of your favorite barbecue sauce
- 8-ounce jar peach preserves

1. In the saucepan, combine the barbecue sauce and peach preserves. Over medium heat, stir the sauce until it begins to simmer. Remove from heat and set aside.

2. In a large mixing bowl, combine beef, pork, eggs, bread crumbs, milk, garlic powder, onion powder, salt, pepper, and red pepper flakes.

3. Mash the mixture with a fork to combine the ingredients. You can use your hands too!

4. Using the 2-inch scoop, portion out scoops of the meat mixture onto the first baking sheet.

5. Shape them into balls by rolling them in a circular pattern between your palms. Place them back on the baking sheet.

6. Heat the oil in a skillet over medium heat. Add a handful of meatballs with about 1 inch of space between each one. Carefully brown all sides of the meatballs. Use tongs to place them on the second, clean baking sheet. Finish browning the remaining meatballs in batches if necessary. Don't worry if they aren't cooked inside. They will finish cooking in the slow cooker.

7   Turn the slow cooker on low. Place the meatballs in the slow cooker and pour the prepared sauce over them. Stir gently until all the meatballs are coated.

8   Cook covered for about 4 hours. Stir occasionally.

9   Place the meatballs on a platter and serve.

15

Dips are the perfect addition to your bowl party. Your party guests will be lining up to spike their crackers, chips, and veggies into your variety of dips.

# GARLICKY HUMMUS

| **PREP TIME** | **20** MINUTES |
|---|---|
| **SERVES** | **6** TO **8** PEOPLE |

## Tools

- colander
- measuring cups
- food processor
- bowl scraper
- cutting board
- chef's knife

## Ingredients

- 2 15-ounce cans chickpeas (garbanzo beans)
- 2 lemons
- ½ cup tahini sauce (sesame seed paste)
- 2 cloves garlic
- 1 teaspoon paprika
- 1 teaspoon salt
- ¼ cup olive oil
- ¼ cup water

**1** Drain the chickpeas in a colander and run cool water over them to rinse.

**2** Place half of the chickpeas in the food processor and turn on high for 30 seconds.

**3** Scrape the edges of the food processor bowl with a bowl scraper so that the chickpeas are at the bottom of the bowl again. Add remaining chickpeas and turn the food processor back on high for an additional 30 seconds.

4 Slice the lemons in half and squeeze the juice directly into the food processor. Catch the seeds if they fall out by holding your hand under the stream of juice.

5 Add remaining ingredients and turn the food processor on high until the mixture is smooth.

6 If the hummus seems a little thick, add 1 tablespoon of water at a time until it is as thick or thin as you prefer.

7 Scrape the hummus into a serving bowl. Serve with pita chips and sliced bell peppers.

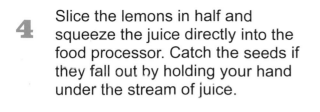

## COACH'S TIP

Don't have a food processor? No problem. A large blender will work too. To make sure you don't give the blender more than it can handle, do steps 2 and 3 in smaller batches.

# FAST AND FRESH SALSA

| | |
|---|---|
| **PREP TIME** | **20** MINUTES |
| **COOK TIME** | **1 HOUR** (INACTIVE) |
| **SERVES** | **6 TO 8** PEOPLE |

## Tools

- chef's knife
- cutting board
- measuring spoons
- large mixing bowl
- spoon

## Ingredients

- **4 Roma tomatoes**
- **1 small red onion**
- **1 jalapeño**
- **½ bunch cilantro**
- **1 teaspoon honey**
- **1 teaspoon salt**
- **1 teaspoon cumin**

1. Chop the tomatoes and red onion. Place in mixing bowl.

2. Seed and slice the jalapeño by slicing lengthwise and scooping the insides firmly with a spoon. Discard seeds. Chop the jalapeño and add to mixing bowl.

3. Pull the leaves off the stems of the cilantro. Don't worry if a few stems end up with the leaves. Push into a small pile and chop into very small pieces.

4. Add remaining ingredients and stir to combine.

5. Allow to stand at room temperature for 1 hour before serving with tortilla chips.

### COACH'S TIP

Don't touch your eyes or face when handling hot peppers like jalapeños! They contain a chemical that may cause a burning sensation. Be sure to wash your hands well when you're done.

# GREAT GUACAMOLE

## Tools

- chef's knife
- cutting board
- kitchen towel
- spoon
- large mixing bowl
- fork
- measuring spoons

| 15 MINUTES | **PREP TIME** |
| 1 HOUR (INACTIVE) | **COOK TIME** |
| 6 TO 8 PEOPLE | **SERVES** |

## Ingredients

- 4 ripe avocados
- 2 limes
- ½ bunch cilantro, chopped
- 1 teaspoon salt
- 1 teaspoon pepper
- 1 clove garlic, minced

1. Have an adult cut the avocados in half and remove the pits. Remove the pits by holding one half in your hand and tapping the blade of the chef's knife on the pit, and then gently twist. Remove the pit from the knife, using a kitchen towel to guard your hand from cuts.

2. Use a spoon to scoop out the avocado flesh from the skin and place it in a large mixing bowl.

3. Slice the limes in half and squeeze the juice into the mixing bowl.

4. Add the remaining ingredients.

5. Use the fork to lightly mash the avocado until it is well blended with the other ingredients.

6. Optional: Add 1 cup of the Fast and Fresh Salsa for additional flavor.

7. Cover the bowl and place in the refrigerator for 1 hour before serving. Serve with tortilla chips and a wedge of lime.

# KICKIN' THREE-BEAN CHILI

Not one, not two, but three kinds of beans give this chili a party-winning kick.

| PREP TIME | 20 MINUTES |
| --- | --- |
| COOK TIME | 1 HOUR |
| SERVES | 8 PEOPLE |

## Tools

- cutting board
- chef's knife
- stockpot
- mixing spoon
- measuring spoons
- can opener

## Ingredients

- 1 tablespoon oil
- 2 bell peppers, chopped
- 2 onions, chopped
- 1 jalapeño, seeds removed and chopped
- 2 pounds lean ground beef
- 2 tablespoons cumin
- ¼ cup chili powder
- 1 teaspoon oregano
- 1 teaspoon paprika
- 1 teaspoon salt
- 1 teaspoon pepper
- ¼ teaspoon cayenne pepper
- 2 15-ounce cans fire-roasted tomatoes, undrained
- 1 15-ounce can black beans, drained
- 1 15-ounce can kidney beans, drained
- 1 15-ounce can pinto beans, drained

Garnishes:
- shredded cheese
- sour cream
- chopped green onions
- crushed tortilla chips

CALL AN AUDIBLE

Want to make this recipe vegetarian? Instead of ground beef, add 2 cups of chopped zucchini, 2 cups of chopped carrots, and 1 cup of chopped eggplant. Reduce the cooking time to 30 minutes.

1 Heat oil over medium heat in a stockpot.

2 Add peppers, onions, and jalapeño to the stockpot and stir. Cook for about 5 minutes, stirring occasionally.

3 Add ground beef and break it up with a mixing spoon. Cook until no longer pink, about 5 to 8 minutes, while stirring occasionally. With an adult's help, drain the fat carefully.

4 Add cumin, chili powder, oregano, paprika, salt, pepper, and cayenne pepper to the pot and stir. Cook for 1 minute.

5 Add tomatoes and beans. Stir all of the ingredients and then reduce heat to medium-low.

6 Simmer for 1 hour. Serve hot in bowls with garnishes.

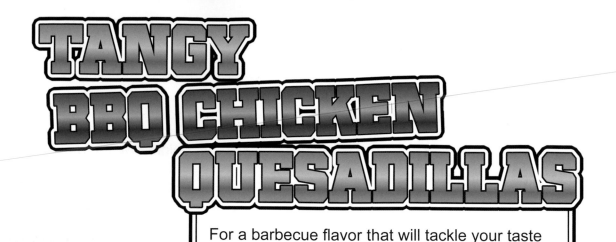

# TANGY BBQ CHICKEN QUESADILLAS

For a barbecue flavor that will tackle your taste buds, try sweet and tangy chicken quesadillas.

**PREP TIME** | **45 MINUTES**

**COOK TIME** | **20 MINUTES**

**SERVES** | **6 TO 8 PEOPLE**

## Tools

- 2 baking sheets
- parchment paper
- cutting board
- chef's knife
- 2 skillets
- measuring cup
- measuring spoons
- spatula
- small mixing bowl
- spoon

## Ingredients

- 2 boneless, skinless chicken breasts
- ½ teaspoon salt
- ¼ teaspoon pepper
- 1 tablespoon oil
- 1 bell pepper, chopped
- 1 small onion, chopped
- ½ tablespoon oil
- ½ cup of your favorite barbecue sauce
- 8 ounces Monterey Jack cheese, shredded
- 4 8-inch flour tortillas

**For the dipping sauce:**
- 1 cup of your favorite barbecue sauce
- ½ cup ranch dressing

1. Preheat oven to 375°F.

2. Line one of the baking sheets with parchment paper. Place the chicken breasts on the parchment paper with at least 2 inches of space between them.

3. Sprinkle salt and pepper on both sides of each breast.

4. Bake the chicken breasts for 25 minutes or until the meat is no longer pink inside.

5. While the chicken is baking, use a skillet to sauté the bell pepper and onion in oil over medium heat until tender. Set aside.

6. When the chicken is done, allow it to cool for about 15 minutes. Then chop the chicken breasts into bite-sized pieces.

7    Turn the oven down to 200°F.

8    Add chicken to the skillet with peppers and onion. Add the barbecue sauce and stir until the ingredients are coated.

9    Add oil to a clean skillet and place one tortilla on the bottom. Put skillet on medium-low heat.

10    Working quickly and carefully, sprinkle on one-fourth of the cheese, leaving about a ½-inch space from the edges.

## CALL AN AUDIBLE

Throwing a grilling football party? These quesadillas are perfect for the grill. Instead of cooking in a skillet, grill the quesadillas over a medium flame for 2 to 3 minutes per side.

11    Place half of the chicken and peppers on top of the cheese. Sprinkle another one-fourth of the cheese on top.

12    Add a tortilla and press down firmly. Allow to cook about 1 to 2 minutes or until golden brown. Using a spatula, flip the quesadilla over carefully and cook an additional 1 to 2 minutes.

13    When finished, place on a clean baking sheet in the oven to keep warm while you make the next one.

14    Repeat steps 9 through 12 for a second quesadilla.

15    Slice the quesadillas into wedges and place on a serving platter.

16    Optional: To make a barbecue ranch dipping sauce, measure the barbecue sauce and ranch dressing into a mixing bowl and stir.

# SLOPPY JOE NACHO BAR

The second quarter just ended, and your guests are hungry. A Sloppy Joe Nacho Bar will make the perfect halftime show!

| PREP TIME | **30** MINUTES |
|---|---|
| COOK TIME | **30** MINUTES |
| SERVES | **6** TO **8** PEOPLE |

## Tools

- cutting board
- chef's knife
- large skillet
- mixing spoon
- measuring cup
- measuring spoons

## Ingredients

- 1 tablespoon oil
- 1 onion, chopped
- 1 red bell pepper, chopped
- 1 green bell pepper, chopped
- 2 cloves garlic, minced
- 2 pounds lean ground beef
- 1 8-ounce can tomato sauce
- 1 cup of your favorite barbecue sauce
- ½ teaspoon dry mustard
- 2 tablespoons Worcestershire sauce
- 1 tablespoon hot sauce
- 1 teaspoon salt
- ½ teaspoon pepper
- 1 12-ounce bag kettle-style potato chips
- 8 ounces cheddar cheese, shredded
- 1 cup bread and butter pickles, roughly chopped
- Optional: 1 cup prepared coleslaw

### COACH'S TIP

You never know when some football fans might show up late to the party. Keep the meat warm for your nacho bar by placing it on the warm setting in a slow cooker.

1. In a large skillet, heat the oil on a medium burner. Add the onion, peppers, and garlic. Cook until slightly softened.

2. Add the ground beef and break the meat into chunks using the mixing spoon. Cook over medium heat until no longer pink. With an adult's help, drain the fat carefully.

3. Add the tomato sauce, barbecue sauce, dry mustard, Worcestershire sauce, hot sauce, salt, and pepper. Turn the heat down to medium-low and simmer for 30 minutes, stirring occasionally.

4. To serve, place chips, meat, cheese, pickles, and coleslaw in separate bowls.

5. Place a layer of chips on each plate, bowl, or container. Then add a couple spoonfuls of meat, followed by cheese, pickles, and coleslaw.

CALL AN AUDIBLE

If you'd rather move the ground beef to the bench, call in 2 pounds of ground turkey or chicken instead.

# PIZZA WAFFLE POCKETS

While you watch your favorite quarterback drop back into the pocket for a pass, grab a breakfast-inspired pocket to enjoy.

| PREP TIME | 30 MINUTES |
| --- | --- |
| COOK TIME | 10 MINUTES |
| MAKES | 16 WAFFLE WEDGES |

## Tools

- waffle iron
- small saucepan
- spoon
- rolling pin
- chef's knife
- measuring cups

## Ingredients

- 2 cups marinara sauce
- all-purpose flour
- 2 13.5-ounce packages refrigerated pizza dough
- cooking spray
- 1 cup mozzarella cheese
- your favorite pizza toppings, such as pepperoni, cooked sausage, or sliced veggies

**1** Preheat the waffle iron.

**2** Place marinara sauce in a small saucepan. Bring to a simmer, then place on low heat and stir occasionally.

**3** Sprinkle some flour onto a clean countertop. Split the pizza dough and, using the rolling pin, roll it into four circles that match the size of your waffle iron. If your waffle iron is rectangular, roll the dough into four rectangle shapes.

**4** Spray the waffle iron lightly with cooking spray.

**5** Place the first circle of pizza dough onto the waffle iron.

**CALL AN AUDIBLE**

Change your pizza waffle pocket into a classic grilled cheese sandwich! Fill the waffle pocket with grated cheddar cheese instead of mozzarella and pizza toppings. Serve with tomato soup to dip.

6 Sprinkle about one-fourth of the cheese over the dough. Then layer your toppings without overcrowding, followed by another one-fourth of the cheese.

7 Carefully place the second dough circle over the top of the cheese and close the waffle iron. Cook for about 3 to 4 minutes or until golden brown.

8 Remove the waffle and slice into eight wedges. Repeat steps for next batch.

9 Serve with warmed marinara sauce for dipping.

# PHILLY CHEESESTEAK SLIDERS

You don't need to be a Philadelphia Eagles fan to fall in love with these sliders!

**PREP TIME** 20 MINUTES

**COOK TIME** 10 MINUTES

**MAKES** 12 SLIDERS

## Tools

- large sauté pan
- measuring spoons
- chef's knife
- cutting board
- measuring cup
- large baking sheet
- tongs

## Ingredients

- 2 tablespoons olive oil
- 1 small onion, sliced thinly
- 1 bell pepper, sliced thinly
- ½ teaspoon salt
- ¼ teaspoon pepper
- 1 pound flank steak, sliced thinly
- ½ cup beef stock or broth
- 12 slider buns
- 12 slices provolone or Monterey Jack cheese

1. In a sauté pan, heat the olive oil over medium heat.

2. Add the sliced peppers and onions. Cook for about 5 minutes or until slightly softened.

3. Season the meat with salt and pepper on both sides. Carefully add the meat to the skillet without splattering. Stir well.

CALL AN AUDIBLE

For a vegetarian alternative, leave out the beef and beef stock. Instead, add 1 pound of mushrooms to step 2. Skip steps 3 through 5.

4 Add the beef stock or broth and turn the heat up to high.

5 Cook the meat for an additional 1 to 2 minutes or until most of the broth is evaporated. Set aside.

6 Open the slider buns and place them on a large baking sheet.

7 Using a tongs, place an equal amount of meat, onion, and pepper on half of all the buns.

8 Place a slice of cheese on top of the meat and place the pan in the oven.

9 Turn on the oven's broil function. Make sure the oven rack is in the highest position. Broil for about 3 minutes or until the cheese is melted and bubbly. Check often to avoid burning.

10 Place bun tops on the sandwiches and serve.

# HAM AND CHEESE PINWHEELS

Team up ham and cheese to set your party spinning with a modern twist on a classic sandwich.

| PREP TIME | **15** MINUTES |
| COOK TIME | **15** MINUTES |
| MAKES | ABOUT **16** PINWHEELS |

## Tools

- large baking sheet
- parchment paper
- mixing bowl
- measuring spoons
- spoon
- bowl scraper
- measuring cup
- chef's knife

## Ingredients

- 2 tablespoons cream cheese, softened
- 1 tablespoon Dijon mustard
- 1 sheet frozen puff pastry, thawed
- 4 ounces sliced deli ham
- 1 cup shredded cheddar or Swiss cheese

1 Preheat oven to 375°F and line a large baking sheet with parchment paper. Set aside.

2 In a mixing bowl, combine cream cheese and Dijon mustard, mixing well.

3 Lay out puff pastry on a clean surface. Evenly spread the cream cheese/Dijon mustard mix with a bowl scraper, leaving a ½-inch space at the top of the pastry.

## CALL AN AUDIBLE

Experiment with various lunch meats and cheeses. Try roast beef and cheddar or turkey and pepper jack cheese. Go vegetarian by substituting the meat with your favorite sliced vegetables.

4 Layer slices of ham to cover the cream cheese/mustard mix.

5 Evenly sprinkle shredded cheese over the ham.

6 Roll the puff pastry from the bottom to the top.

7 Slice into 16 equal pieces and place on the large baking sheet with about 2 inches between each pinwheel.

8 Bake for 15 to 18 minutes or until golden brown.

9 Allow to cool slightly before serving.

# CHOCOLATE-DIPPED FOOTBALL STRAWBERRIES

Your guests will be rushing to get their hands on the ball—sweet and succulent football strawberries, that is!

| | |
|---|---|
| **PREP TIME** | **10** MINUTES |
| **COOK TIME** | **30** MINUTES |
| **MAKES** | ABOUT **25** STRAWBERRIES |

## Tools

- large baking sheet
- parchment paper
- measuring cup
- 2 microwave-safe bowls
- spoon

## Ingredients

- 1 pound strawberries
- 8 ounces semisweet chocolate chips
- 1 0.68-ounce tube decorating gel

## CALL AN AUDIBLE

It's easy to make inside-out football strawberries! Substitute white chocolate for the semisweet chocolate, and pipe the laces with brown gel.

1 Wash and pat strawberries dry. Set aside.

2 Line a large baking sheet with parchment paper.

3 Put the semisweet chocolate chips into a bowl. Melt the chocolate chips by microwaving at 10 percent power. Microwave 30 seconds at a time until the chocolate chips are completely melted, stirring in between.

4 Hold the stem of a strawberry and dip into the melted chocolate, as close to the stem as you can. Hold the strawberry above the bowl and allow the excess chocolate to drip off before placing it on the parchment-lined baking sheet. Repeat for all the berries.

5 Place sheet of dipped berries in the refrigerator to harden for about 10 minutes.

6 Leaving the berries on the parchment paper, carefully pipe football laces with the decorating gel onto the chocolate by squeezing the tube.

7 Allow the chocolate and gel to continue to harden for about 30 minutes in the refrigerator before serving.

# S'MORES SKILLET

No fireplace? No problem. You don't need a fire to make this delicious treat!

| | |
|---|---|
| **PREP TIME** | **15** MINUTES |
| **COOK TIME** | **15** MINUTES |
| **SERVES** | **8** PEOPLE |

## Tools

- measuring cup
- medium cast-iron or oven-safe skillet

## Ingredients

- 2 12-ounce bags milk chocolate chips
- 2 cups mini marshmallows
- 1 14-ounce box graham crackers, for dipping

## CALL AN AUDIBLE

Add some variety to your S'mores Skillet by offering various dipper options, such as vanilla wafer cookies, cinnamon pita chips, or apples.

1 Preheat oven to 450°F.

2 Place the chocolate chips in the bottom of the skillet. Add the marshmallows.

3 Place in oven and bake for 8 to 10 minutes or until the marshmallows turn golden brown. Check often to avoid burning.

4 Carefully remove from oven and serve in the skillet with graham crackers on the side.

# CHOCOLATEY FRUITY MINI PIZZAS

Watch your guests start to huddle around you as you hand off tasty dessert mini pizzas.

| PREP TIME | 15 MINUTES |
|---|---|
| COOK TIME | 15 MINUTES |
| MAKES | 16 MINI PIZZAS |

## Tools

- mixing bowl
- bowl scraper
- measuring cup
- chef's knife
- cutting board

## Ingredients

- 16 sugar cookies, prepared
- ½ cup cream cheese, softened to room temperature
- ½ cup chocolate hazelnut spread
- 1 cup strawberries
- 1 banana
- 2 kiwis
- ½ cup blueberries

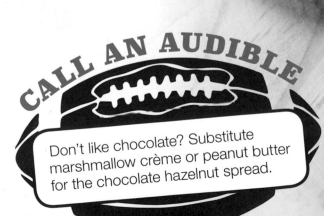

## CALL AN AUDIBLE

Don't like chocolate? Substitute marshmallow crème or peanut butter for the chocolate hazelnut spread.

1. In a mixing bowl, mix the cream cheese and chocolate hazelnut spread with a bowl scraper.

2. Slice strawberries, banana, and kiwis into bite-sized pieces.

3. Spread about 1 tablespoon of the cream cheese mixture on each cookie with a bowl scraper.

4. Decorate with fruit and serve.

**COACH'S TIP**
You don't have to stick with the fruits listed here. Get creative! Choose fruits with colors of your favorite teams to show your team pride.

# COOKIE BITES

Your guests won't be fumbling these ooey-gooey, bite-sized cookie bites!

| PREP TIME | **10** MINUTES |
|---|---|
| COOK TIME | **10** MINUTES |
| MAKES | **25** COOKIE BITES |

## Tools

- food processor
- measuring cup
- mixing bowl
- spoon
- microwave-safe bowl
- two forks
- large baking sheet
- parchment paper

## Ingredients

- 8 ounces of your favorite cookies
- 4 ounces cream cheese, softened to room temperature
- 1 cup white or milk chocolate chips
- decorating icing or gel (optional)

1. Place cookies in the food processor and pulse until the cookies are mostly crumbled. Measure out ¼ cup of the crumbs and set aside. Transfer the remaining crumbs (should be about ¾ cup) to a mixing bowl.

2. Add the cream cheese and mix well. Using a spoon, measure out about 25 pieces. Then roll them in between your palms to make a ball shape. Set aside.

## COACH'S TIP

If you don't have a food processor, simply place the cookies in a resealable plastic bag. Press the air out, seal the bag, and pound it with a mallet or rolling pin until you make crumbs.

**3** In the microwave, melt the chocolate chips at 10 percent power in 30-second intervals until melted.

**4** Using two forks, pinch the ball and drop it in the bowl of chocolate. Roll the ball around until it is covered. Place on a baking sheet lined with parchment paper.

**5** After you've dipped all the balls, take the reserved crumbs and sprinkle over the top.

**6** Place the baking sheet in the fridge to harden the chocolate for about 30 minutes.

**7** Optional: Use decorating icing or gel to create designs or logos.

CALL AN AUDIBLE

While you're rolling the mixture in step 2, shape the balls into helmets instead. Use kitchen shears to cut ropes of licorice into small segments. Attach them to the helmets after step 5 to create face masks.

# PEANUT BUTTER CHOCOLATE PRETZEL STICKS

Pretzel sticks are in double coverage! Both peanut butter and chocolate smother the handheld treats.

| PREP TIME | 10 MINUTES |
|---|---|
| COOK TIME | 15 MINUTES |
| MAKES | 10 PRETZEL STICKS |

## Tools

- large baking sheet
- parchment paper
- shallow microwave-safe dish
- bowl scraper

## Ingredients

- 1 cup chocolate chips
- ½ cup peanut butter
- 10 pretzel rods
- toppings such as chopped nuts, sprinkles, and shredded coconut

## COACH'S TIP

The chocolate might begin to harden in the bowl while you're dipping the pretzels. Instead of fighting through thick chocolate, simply microwave the chocolate for 10 to 15 seconds to melt it again.

1 Line a baking sheet with parchment paper. Set aside.

2 In the microwave-safe dish, melt the chocolate and peanut butter together at 10 percent power in 30-second intervals until melted. Stir to combine.

3 Hold one end of the pretzel rod and dip the other end in the chocolate about two-thirds of the way up the pretzel. You can use a bowl scraper to help apply chocolate to the pretzel.

4 Place on a parchment-lined baking sheet and immediately sprinkle with toppings. Repeat for the remaining pretzel rods. Allow to cool for about two hours before serving.

**PREP TIME** | **5 MINUTES**

**SERVES** | **8 PEOPLE**

Three colorful punches provide tasty options to keep your guests from becoming thirsty while cheering during the game!

# GINGER-PINEAPPLE PUNCH

## Tools

- measuring cup
- punch bowl or large beverage dispenser
- long-handled spoon

## Ingredients

- 2 liters ginger ale
- 1 liter pineapple juice
- 1 12-ounce container frozen limeade concentrate, thawed
- ice, for serving

**1** In the punch bowl or beverage dispenser, combine the ginger ale, pineapple juice, and limeade concentrate. Stir well.

**2** Place in the refrigerator for 3 hours to cool or serve immediately with ice.

# CREAMY ORANGE POPSICLE PUNCH

## Tools

- punch bowl
- ice cream scoop
- measuring cup
- long-handled spoon

## Ingredients

- 1 pint orange sherbet
- 1 pint vanilla ice cream or frozen yogurt
- 2 liters cream soda
- 2 liters orange soda

# TRIPLE-BERRY LEMONADE

## Tools

- food processor or blender
- punch bowl or large beverage dispenser
- long-handled spoon

## Ingredients

- 1 12-ounce bag frozen berry mix, thawed
- 2 liters lemon-lime soda
- 2 liters ginger ale
- 1 12-ounce container frozen lemonade concentrate, thawed
- ice, for serving

1 Place the berries in the food processor or blender. Blend well.

2 Combine both sodas, lemonade concentrate, and blended berries in the punch bowl or dispenser and stir well.

3 Place in refrigerator for 3 hours or serve immediately with ice.

1 Using the ice cream scoop, place the ice cream and sherbet in a punch bowl.

2 Add the cream soda and orange soda. Stir well before serving.

# BRATWURST PRETZEL SLIDERS

Timeout! Are you ready to tackle delicious bratwurst pretzel sliders? Wow your fans with this game-winning recipe.

**PREP TIME** | **1 HOUR** (30 MINUTES INACTIVE)

**COOK TIME** | **30 MINUTES**

**MAKES** | **12 SLIDERS**

## Tools

- saucepan
- three mixing bowls
- measuring cups
- measuring spoons
- damp kitchen towel
- chef's knife
- large stockpot
- fork
- slotted spoon
- large baking sheet
- parchment paper
- whisk
- pastry brush
- large sauté pan

## Ingredients

**For the dough:**
- 2 tablespoons butter
- 1 packet instant yeast
- 1 pinch of salt
- 1 teaspoon honey
- 1 cup warm water
- 2½ cups flour, plus more for kneading
- vegetable oil spray

**For cooking:**
- 3 cups water
- ½ cup baking soda
- 1 egg
- 6 fresh bratwurst
- 1 tablespoon olive oil
- 1 onion, thinly sliced
- salt and pepper
- 1 recipe Honey-Mustard Dipping Sauce (see page 9)
- sauerkraut (optional)

### For the pretzel buns:

**1** Place the butter in a saucepan and melt over low heat.

**2** In a large mixing bowl, combine the yeast, salt, melted butter, honey, and warm water. Allow to sit for about 2 minutes.

**3** Add the flour. Mix it well and turn the bowl of dough onto a floured surface. Knead it well with your hands for about 5 minutes, or until it is soft and smooth.

**4** Spray the inside of a clean mixing bowl with vegetable oil spray and place the dough in the bowl. Cover with a clean damp cloth and allow to sit for 30 minutes to rise.

**5** Flour your surface again and place the dough ball on it. Knead for 1 minute and then cut the dough into 12 equal pieces.

**6** Pour the 3 cups water into the large stockpot. Add baking soda and bring to a boil. Reduce heat to simmer.

**7** Sprinkle some flour on a clean counter and roll the dough chunks into balls by rolling the dough in the palm of your hand against the counter. Make sure the dough is smooth all over. Repeat with the remaining dough.

**8** Carefully drop four dough balls into the boiling water/baking soda mixture and simmer for about 30 seconds on one side. Then carefully flip using a fork and simmer for an additional 30 seconds. While the dough simmers, line the baking sheet with parchment paper.

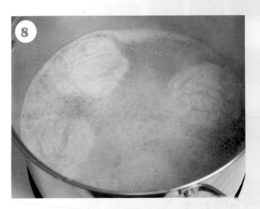

**9** Remove the dough with a slotted spoon and place on the parchment paper. Repeat with remaining dough.

**10** Whisk the egg in a small mixing bowl. Using a pastry brush, gently paint the top surface of each bun with the egg wash.

**11** Carefully score the top of the buns with your chef's knife by marking an X.

**12** Sprinkle with salt and bake for 15 to 18 minutes or until the buns are a deep golden brown. Remove and set aside to cool.

**13** Slice in half horizontally.

## For the bratwurst burgers:

**1** Carefully score the casing of the bratwurst lengthwise. Peel the casing off and discard.

**2** Cut each sausage link in half. Use your hands to form the meat into 12 patties.

**3** Heat olive oil in a large sauté pan over medium heat and add the sliced onions. Stir. Sprinkle a little salt and pepper in the pan. Cook until the onions are softened and slightly golden brown. Remove from pan and set aside.

**4** Using the same pan, turn the heat to medium and add the bratwurst patties, working in batches if necessary. Cook for about 3 to 4 minutes per side, or until each side is browned and cooked in the middle.

**To assemble:**

1  Open the pretzel bun and place a bratwurst burger on the bottom. Add about 2 tablespoons of onion. You can also add sauerkraut on top of the onions.

2  Spread 1 tablespoon of the honey mustard on the inside of the top half of the pretzel bun. Serve on a platter. Now you're cooking like a pro!

# READ MORE

**Besel, Jen.** *Sugarcoat It! Desserts to Design, Decorate, and Devour.* North Mankato, Minn.: Capstone Press, 2015.

**Gold, Rozanne.** *Eat Fresh Food: Awesome Recipes for Teen Chefs.* New York: Bloomsbury Children's Books, 2009.

**Meachen Rau, Dana.** *A Teen Guide to Creative, Delightful Dinners.* North Mankato, Minn.: Compass Point Books, 2011.

**Pellman Good, Phyllis.** *Fix-It and Forget-It Kids' Cookbook: 50 Favorite Recipes to Make in a Slow Cooker.* Intercourse, Pa.: Good Books, 2010.

# INTERNET SITES

FactHound offers a safe, fun way to find Internet sites related to this book. All of the sites on FactHound have been researched by our staff.

Here's all you do:

Visit *www.facthound.com*

Type in this code: 9781491421369

**About the Author**

Katrina Jorgensen is a graduate of Le Cordon Bleu College of Culinary Arts. She enjoys creating new recipes and sharing them with friends and family. She lives in Rochester, Minnesota, with her husband, Tony, and dog, Max.